God of Miracles

Sue Collins

Onwards and Upwards Publishers

3 Radfords Turf
Cranbrook
Exeter
EX5 7DX
United Kingdom
www.onwardsandupwards.org

This first edition published in the United Kingdom by Onwards and Upwards Publishers (2017).

ISBN: 978-1-911086-88-8
Typeface: Sabon LT
Editor: Victoria Lyle
Graphic design: LM Graphic Design

Printed in the United Kingdom.

Endorsements

In all good stories, the main characters have to go through awful trials to find two things: firstly, the will to overcome and secondly, keeping their vision on the future prize. In this story you will find three heroes who face awful trials yet find the will and the vision with grace.

Sue has written with heart-rending reality of the pain, the hope, the disappointments and the faith that keeps enduring that she and her husband Phil faced. This story will make you cry but it will also help you to hope, to pray, to press on to a better day in whatever trial you face.

But I said three heroes. The third is Jesus, their Lord and Saviour. He is the centre of their lives and it was He who kept them and ultimately blessed them. It is the suffering of Jesus that inspired them; it will inspire you.

For myself, I admire this lovely couple and I am so pleased they wrote this story, their story. I warn you that you will weep. But you will also rejoice.

A good story. A true story. An eternal story.

Paul Johnson
Retired New Frontiers church leader

We all have hopes and aspirations in our life, but none so important as those we have for our children. From the first cry our lives are changed forever. This book is about Phil and Sue, their children and the God of miracles.

We have known Phil from a child and Sue almost as long as they have been together. They are a quiet, reserved, hardworking, uncomplicated couple who love Jesus. They were part of our church family for many years and also our own family, our four children and us.

When it was time for them to start their own family, we were thrilled and shared in their preparations for family life. We felt they would be 'good' parents, with Christian values and an abundance of love.

This book is the story of the outworking of all that they are as a couple, a family and their complete trust in the Living God. We count it a privilege to have been part of this testimony and their lives.

Pastor Peter and Mary Cook

About the Author

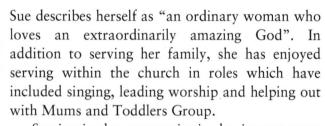 Sue describes herself as "an ordinary woman who loves an extraordinarily amazing God". In addition to serving her family, she has enjoyed serving within the church in roles which have included singing, leading worship and helping out with Mums and Toddlers Group.

Serving in the community is also important to Sue and she has listened to children read in school, helped with a parenting course and, as a qualified Counsellor, worked with the Kent Christian counselling service 'Crossline' before her recent move to the Midlands with her husband.

Sue's hobbies include various kinds of craftwork, playing guitar and reading. She loves spending quality time with her husband, family and friends.

To contact Sue Collins, please write to:
collins.godofmiracles@gmail.com

Or connect with her on Facebook:
www.facebook.com/susanjcollins64

Contents

God of Miracles

Foreword by Elisabeth Newman

As a founder member and Co-ordinator of Crossline Christian Counselling Service in Maidstone for twenty-three years, I have interviewed many applicants wanting to counsel within our organisation.

When in 2009 Sue applied for a placement as a trainee counsellor, there was something that stood out in her interview. It was as if she had the word 'counsellor' written on her forehead. Her gentle character and her desire to depend on God for wisdom when seeing clients were, among other attributes, confirmation that she would be a suitable candidate. We were very happy to offer her the position needed for her Diploma in Counselling.

As Sue's Supervisor for part of her time in Crossline, I got to know her quite well. When she had shared some of her experiences with me, I was not surprised that God had called her into Christian counselling.

Sue's story makes compulsive reading as she honestly relates tragedies and victories; a 'must read', particularly for those experiencing suffering as this can give hope and encouragement. God still performs miracles, as is evident from this testimony.

Elisabeth Newman
Retired Coordinator of Crossline Christian Counselling Service
Author of "My Strong Tower"

God of Miracles

CHAPTER ONE

Christopher Roy Collins

I was twenty-four years old when I left my full-time job as an Insurance Documentation Technician for the Corporation of Lloyd's (Chatham office) to begin my maternity leave. It was a time of great joy for me, as I had always strongly desired to be a mother. Philip and I had been married for just under four years and, having moved to a three-bedroom house from our one-bedroom maisonette two years earlier, we now felt ready to start a family of our own.

Other than for morning sickness and a minor bleed early on in the pregnancy, I had been in good health throughout and had no reason to doubt that in a few weeks I would go into labour and have a strong, healthy baby.

On my final day at work, I walked around the various departments saying farewell to colleagues and offering the customary tin of sweets. I was full of joy and excitement about becoming a mum for the first time. I had felt spoilt and special as friends had pinned a beautiful, fragrant corsage of freesias onto me and showered me with their good wishes and generous gifts for the baby. I felt blessed and happy. However, by the time I had finished my tour and said my goodbyes, I also felt a sense of unease brought about by a few comments made by some of the female staff. Some were surprised I was leaving already as I didn't look that far along in my pregnancy. Others said my bump was rather small and one of them asked if I was taking maternity leave early. I tried to push the comments from my mind, telling myself that the midwife would have noticed if there was a problem.

As I left the building and waited at my sister Jackie's home for Phil to collect me and the lovely assortment of baby gifts, the comments kept replaying in my mind and the sense of unease turned into anxiety.

Later that evening, as I discussed my anxious thoughts with Phil, we tried to rationalise the possible reasons why I didn't look as pregnant as other mums at this stage: I was a petite build, maybe it was the position the baby was lying in, maybe some had more fluid around the baby, some people gain more weight than others, etc. On the surface I comforted myself with these seemingly rational thoughts but, as I prepared the home for the baby's arrival, on a deeper level a small seed of doubt was still niggling away.

At thirty-six weeks pregnant, I attended my routine antenatal appointment with the local midwife. We went through the standard checks as usual: weight, blood pressure, urine sample and baby's heart rate. At the end of the examination, the midwife expressed her concern over some of her findings. My blood pressure was high, there was protein in my urine sample and my ankles were swollen. As these were all symptoms of pre-eclampsia, she said I needed to go to the hospital to be checked there. She suggested I go as soon as possible and that I take an overnight bag.

At the hospital, the obstetric consultant confirmed the diagnosis of pre-eclampsia and I was admitted to a ward. I didn't really understand the dangers associated with pre-eclampsia and, because I was feeling well, believed that I would soon be sent home. My baby wasn't due for almost four weeks and the idea I would be in hospital that long or I would give birth earlier simply didn't cross my mind.

There was a pleasant atmosphere of camaraderie on the antenatal section of the ward; mums chatted happily about babies' names, whether they hoped for a boy or a girl, whether they planned to bottle-feed or breastfeed, etc. To pass the time, we read magazines, knitted for our babies and watched TV in the day room. There were regular checks on our blood pressure and the babies' heartbeats were monitored a few times each day. I felt quite relaxed and soon got used to the daily routines of the ward. However, that changed when I encountered a patient from the postnatal section of the ward.

As I was walking down the corridor towards the bathroom, I came across a lady I had not seen before. We stopped and exchanged a few comments about the ward and then she asked me whether I had had a boy or a girl (scans were still quite new then and radiographers were unable to reliably identify gender). I was rather taken aback by her question, but managed to reply jovially that I was still expecting. She apologised and, when I had asked about her baby, I returned to my bed.

As I walked back, memories of my last day at work flooded back to me. This time there was no trying to rationalise the comment away and I started to feel anxious as I tried to take in the reality of my situation. I was in hospital, I had pre-eclampsia and, although I was nearly thirty-seven weeks pregnant, I didn't look it.

As I had been admitted on the Friday evening of the May Day bank holiday, there was no ward round until the Tuesday morning. The obstetric registrar examined me and then queried the length of my pregnancy with the ward sister accompanying her. She was astounded when the sister confirmed I was over thirty-six weeks. The registrar questioned why it had not been noted before now that the baby was very small. She explained to me that due to the pre-eclampsia and the baby's size, I might need to have my labour induced. However, she said that I was in the right place and that they would continue to monitor the baby and see how things went.

As the doctor left, I felt an odd mixture of emotions. I felt naturally anxious about what I had been told, and yet there was also a relief that a doctor had seen and confirmed the problem. At the same time, I also felt a naïve excitement at the prospect of having my baby sooner.

The following afternoon, the registrar returned to examine me again. She said that she felt it best to induce my labour the following day because there was no improvement in my condition or the readings of the baby's heart rate.

The next morning, all my belongings were placed on a trolley and I moved to the labour ward. As the labour was not 'normal', I was taken to one of the two clinical delivery rooms. When we had looked around during our antenatal classes, we had seen the regular delivery rooms, which were quite homely. This room was equipped for medical purposes only and the equipment and things around me left me with a sense of foreboding.

The nurses were lovely and tried hard to put me at ease. I was connected to a drip via a needle inserted into the back of my hand to induce labour, and a nurse attempted to break my waters for me. However, when she went to do so, the baby was already showing signs of distress and was passing meconium (a black sticky substance from the baby's bowel, normally passed soon after birth). After some unpleasant attempts with the waters, the nurses concluded that I had had very little by way of water around the baby and that what I did have had dispersed the previous evening.

The labour was rapid for an induction, taking under six hours. The baby was monitored throughout and was in distress. As I got to the second stage of labour, the doctors were called because the midwife was concerned that I needed an emergency caesarean section. This was because pushing the baby out could have caused a fatal reduction in his heart rate / oxygen level. In order to assess the condition of the baby quickly, they told me that they needed to get a blood sample from the baby's head. All I wanted to do at that stage was push, but I had to wait while the procedure to get the blood from the baby was carried out. Fortunately, the oxygen levels in the blood were sufficient for me to continue and I was then encouraged by the sister to put everything I had into pushing the baby out as quickly as possible.

Christopher Roy was born quickly and, although small, appeared to be perfectly healthy. The nurses thought he weighed around 5 lbs and so left us alone with him to rush to an emergency elsewhere on the ward. When they returned and weighed him at 3 lbs 12 ozs, a team was called from the special care baby unit (SCBU). Although he was quite long, he was very skinny and had been slowly starving in the womb due to poor blood flow through the placenta. When the placenta was delivered, rather than being a healthy red organ the size of a dinner plate, it was small, shrivelled and greyish white in appearance. I was told it had calcified. Placentas can become like this when mothers smoke heavily during pregnancy. When the nursing auxiliary saw the placenta, she made a comment about me being a smoker. I was astounded and upset, as I had never smoked.

When he arrived in SCBU, Christopher was weak and unable to suck, so he had to be fed via a nasal gastric tube. Each time a new tube was put down his nose into his stomach, the nurse had to check it had gone into the stomach and not the lung. To do this, the nurse would draw up some fluid from the stomach. One day we watched her carry out this procedure and she drew up blood. Immediately, Christopher was wheeled into the intensive care section of the ward and doctors surrounded him. We were told that the blood could indicate a serious problem. However, after further tests the next day, he was returned to the main room on the ward. When he was ten days old, Christopher was feeding well, weighed 4 lbs and was discharged from hospital.

Many babies were born prematurely at that time and had a few problems before they went home. However, it is significant that there was a serious problem with my pregnancy that had gone undetected and untreated for some weeks before the birth. As the rest of my story unfolds, the significance of Christopher surviving his birth will hopefully seem as extraordinary to you as it did to us. Christopher was very likely to have been a stillborn baby who died in the womb due to lack of oxygen resulting from poor blood flow through the placenta.

CHAPTER TWO

Nathan John Collins

The following year, I was expecting our second child, due to be born in late September, when Christopher would be just sixteen months old. We had not planned to have children so close together, but were thrilled when we discovered I was pregnant again.

As the pregnancy progressed, I felt increasingly tired and irritable and by the fifth month I was struggling to cope with the daily demands of a lively toddler and normal household activities. One afternoon I found myself struggling to get Christopher ready to go out for a routine midwife appointment. There was quite a wait at the surgery and looking after Christopher and getting him in and out of his pushchair was almost too much for me. I felt out of sorts and tearful with the effort of it all.

At the end of my examination, I was told that my blood pressure was very high, my ankles were swollen and that I had protein in my urine specimen. The midwife said that I needed to go to hospital straight away, at which point I burst into tears. Apparently, pre-eclampsia was rare in second pregnancies and I was unfortunate to have had it with both. The midwife was kind and reassuring and I was offered the phone to contact Phil and arrange to be taken in. He in turn arranged for his mum to collect Christopher.

As with my first pregnancy, I was admitted to the maternity ward, only this time I was thirty weeks pregnant and had another ten weeks to go! Knowing that Christopher had been delivered within a week of being admitted, I was worried that this baby would be too early. I remained in hospital with high blood pressure and an increasing amount of protein in my urine, which eventually reached the highest amount measurable. I spent the first few days on the ward with other mums, but as things got worse, I was moved to a room of my own near to the nurses' station. I was ignorant of the fact that they were concerned I could develop full-blown eclampsia, which could be fatal for me and possibly my baby. Unlike the time leading up to when Christopher was born, I actually felt ill.

The baby's heartbeat was monitored two or three times a day by a machine that produced a printout for the doctor to look at. On the Sunday afternoon, while Phil was visiting and I was attached to the monitor, the sound of the heartbeat slowed considerably and the graph on the printout dipped to the bottom and along flat for a second before gradually climbing a bit further up. I knew that readings sometimes did strange things if one of the sensors on my bump slipped and was not touching properly. However, I had not been moving around and could see that it was as it should be. Feeling suddenly anxious, we called the nurse to come and check the graph. Once she had done this, it seemed as if everything went into fast forward with staff rushing around and in and out of my room. They were talking between themselves with hushed voices, and worried expressions were visible on their faces. I realised that whatever was happening was serious and our anxiety level rose.

We were told that the baby was distressed and in danger and that they needed to perform a C-section to deliver the baby as soon as possible. Blood was taken and I was prepared for surgery. Then everything went strangely quiet. We were eventually told that they would not be able to deliver the baby after all, due to the fact it was Sunday and there was not a suitable paediatric specialist available for the baby, who would need intensive care.

I can say without any hesitation that night was the longest and most difficult of my life, up to then. When Phil eventually had to leave, I was left alone in my room with the knowledge that at any moment there might be an unmonitored repeat of what we had seen earlier and that my baby's heart might stop without anyone knowing until it was too late. We had prayed together before Phil went home and I knew that others would be praying that night. However, once alone in my room with the ward settled down for the night, I felt as if my faith was being drained out of me and I began to feel desperately afraid. I knew that my blood pressure was very high and I began to worry that the stress of the events that afternoon plus the waiting had pushed it up further. I tried to will myself to be still and calm, but my spirit was paralysed by the fear that in this anxious condition I might actually kill my baby or both of us with eclampsia before the morning. I felt an overwhelming sense of being responsible.

Then, as if prompted, I knew what to do. I couldn't fight this battle alone, so I put on my dressing gown and walked off the ward to the reception foyer where the public phones were located. I dialled my pastor's number and, with difficulty, due to the tears that were already flowing, asked to speak to his wife, Mary. I don't recall how long I was on the phone, but I do remember her bringing words of comfort and prayers that were like a balm to me. As we talked and prayed, the lies and the fear began to subside and the truth broke through. I was not responsible for what was happening to my body. I was sick, but I could place the baby into God's care. He or she belonged to Him too and He had knit this little one together in my womb. I was reminded of Psalm 139 verses 13 to 16, which say:

> *"For You created my inmost being;*
> *You knit me together in my mother's womb.*
> *I praise You because I am fearfully and wonderfully made;*
> *Your works are wonderful,*
> *I know that full well.*
> *My frame was not hidden from You*
> *When I was made in the secret place.*
> *When I was woven together in the depths of the earth,*
> *Your eyes saw my unformed body.*
> *All the days ordained for me were written in Your book*
> *Before one of them came to be."*

I returned to my room feeling very peaceful and my spirit was refreshed. The voice of the enemy had abated.

The following day I was taken to the operating theatre and Nathan John was born by C-section. He weighed just 2 lbs 4 ozs and was taken straight to the SCBU. As he had been delivered under general anaesthetic, I was unable to see him, but a photo taken by the nurses was placed by my bed.

In the early hours of the following morning, I woke to find a doctor, whom I had not seen before, beside my bed putting up another drip. As I woke and looked groggily up at him, he told me not to worry. He explained that he was a renal (kidney) doctor and told me that I had suffered kidney failure, which he was dealing with. He reassured me and suggested I try to go back to sleep.

Despite having been so ill, I was determined to see Nathan and, on the second day, I was taken to SCBU in a wheelchair to see him for the first time. He was in a heated cot that, unlike the full incubators, didn't have a lid. However, he had a small plastic box inside the cot that covered his head. We were told that he was having a little bit of trouble with his breathing and that a small amount of oxygen was being fed into the box.

I could only manage short visits due to my own health, but we went to see Nathan again before Phil went home that evening. We visited him together again before Phil had to leave for home that evening. Two nurses were listening to his chest when we walked in and he had a tiny bit of bubbly saliva in one of the corners of his mouth. They moved away and left us to say goodnight to our tiny son, returning to his side as soon as we left the room. Just as we were leaving the ward, I had an impulse to take photos of Nathan. Maybe, on an unconscious level, I was worried by what I had seen. I mentioned taking photos to Phil but, as we were both very tired, we agreed to wait until the morning. As far as we knew, there was nothing to worry about, so Phil went home and I went back to the ward.

I had great difficulty sleeping that night because I was suffering with abdominal cramps. I was told that it was common after C-sections and that it was nothing to worry about. The pain was caused by trapped air created by the moving of the colon during the operation. I had hardly slept when a nurse came back into my room around 1 am. She said that Nathan needed me and that the staff in SCBU had asked me to go up there.

As I arrived in the baby unit, there were nurses and a doctor surrounding Nathan. One of the nurses was 'bagging' him, which meant she was pushing the air in and out of him with a piece of apparatus, and another was keeping his heart pumping. Instantly, I knew he was in real trouble. The young female doctor put her arm around me and, with tears in her eyes, said she was so sorry but his lung had haemorrhaged and there was nothing more she could do for him. The doctors had been monitoring him carefully, but his condition had deteriorated suddenly and catastrophically.

The doctor asked if it was OK with me for them to stop working on Nathan. I was in shock and felt unable to make that decision. I desperately wanted Phil to see our son again before we let him go and I wanted us to make the decision together. The staff said that they would phone Phil and speak to him for me or I could ring him myself. So, with great difficulty, I did and, between the sobs, told him what had happened. We talked for a couple of minutes. I told him that I couldn't let Nathan go until he had come; that I couldn't make the decision for the staff to stop CPR. At this point, knowing I was stuck and distressed, Phil bravely put aside his own desire to see Nathan one more time, and made the hard decision to allow staff to stop before he arrived. He knew that it would take him at least thirty minutes to get to the ward and was aware of the impact that waiting for him would have on Nathan, me and the doctor and nurses. He explained this gently to me and once I understood his concerns, I was in agreement that this was for the best. It was the hardest decision to make, because we both desperately wanted to say goodbye to our son together.

Nathan looked so helpless and tiny, his blue eyes looking up at me. I instinctively put my hands upon him and prayed. However, I have no reliable memory as to whether I asked God to heal him. I do vividly remember that in his last moments I thanked God for giving him to us for such a short time and asked Him to take our tiny son home and out of suffering. I said goodbye to him and let him go to be with Jesus. At that point in my life it was the hardest thing that I had ever had to do and I felt so alone. Our baby was just two-and-a-half days old.

Nathan was placed in a Moses basket by a nurse, and together we made our way to a small room to wait for Phil, who was being driven in by his dad. At the same time, our pastor, Peter Cook, was also on his way, accompanied by one of the church elders. As the nurse carried him there, the whole sequence of events seemed dream-like to me, as if this wasn't really happening.

I was desperate to protect my husband from the distressing things I had seen and, because Nathan's little blue eyes were still gazing up at me, I asked the nurse to close them so that he looked peacefully asleep. Sometime before Phil arrived, Nathan was taken to another room. My memory is very hazy about this, but I think I was distressed and in shock and someone asked whether I would like Nathan moved. I was grieving and yet somehow I had coped with all I needed to do. At that time I would not have described myself as a strong person and yet God gave me strength.

When Phil arrived at the hospital, he first spent time with me and then went to see Nathan. One of the biggest emotional hurdles for him was finding our little son in the Moses basket in one of the ward's utility areas. He had wanted and expected to find Nathan with me and thought we would spend a little time together before we said goodbye to him. He was deeply wounded that his little boy had been left alone. The way in which Nathan's body was dealt with that night seemed to be a rushed and poorly managed affair and the staff seemed unable to pre-empt what was needed or to realise that finding your deceased baby alone in a utility area was distressing.

When we returned to the maternity ward, there was further upset. Whilst we had been in the SCBU, all my things had been transferred to another room. The new room had two beds, so it was possible for Phil to spend the night in hospital with me, which was good, but it had been poorly managed again. It felt cold and impersonal for staff to move my things so quickly and without suggesting it to us first.

As I was still a patient, recovering from a C-section, I had to stay in hospital until the surgical clips holding my wound together could be removed and I was well enough to return home. This was really hard and it meant I was unable to go with Phil to register Nathan's birth and death. I asked for the clips to be taken out as soon as possible. The nurse removing the clips said that ideally she would recommend them staying in one or two days longer. However, she was sympathetic to my desire to leave hospital and therefore began removing them. A couple of the clips were difficult to get out and the procedure was very uncomfortable. Following my discharge from the hospital, I developed an infection in the wound.

Although I had wanted to leave hospital quickly, when the day finally came it was very difficult. All the other mothers, on being discharged, walked down to the main entrance escorted by a smiling midwife carrying their new arrival. Once in the foyer, the nurse would hand the baby into the arms of the mother or father and say farewell. We walked alone and we left with empty arms. It was devastating. I had given birth, and had the physical effects of a C-section to bear, but our baby was never coming home.

The post-mortem said that Nathan had died due to his prematurity and growth retardation caused by poor blood flow through the placenta (placental insufficiency). He had developed hyaline membrane disease that resulted in a lung haemorrhage, which was a common cause of death in premature babies at this time. They were born before the natural lubricants (surfactants) had developed in their lungs; therefore, the lungs were prone to sticking together inside, preventing proper lung function. As in Nathan's case, the lung was prone to pop or haemorrhage.

Following Nathan's death, we went to stay with Phil's parents who lived just a few miles away from our home. This meant that Christopher could be cared for whilst I recovered sufficiently, physically and emotionally, to be able to return home. The day of the funeral came and we were driven to the crematorium by Phil's parents. We followed the funeral director's car containing the tiny white coffin. As we entered the chapel, Brahms' lullaby played softly and our little boy's coffin was placed at the front of the room. Phil and I had decided beforehand that we would try to be brave during the service for Nathan, so that we could take on board what was said and remember it. I think this was a desperate attempt to hold on to every little memory connected with our son's short life. I tried hard to fight back the tide of emotion that crashed in upon me that day and waited for the time when we were alone later that day to share our tears and comfort one another.

At the funeral, I was completely unprepared for the reactions and responses of others and found it hard to comprehend their grief. I had felt that this was a very private and personal loss for Phil and me. Due to the shortness of his life, virtually no-one had had the opportunity to see Nathan. In retrospect, I have wondered whether this was responsible for some of the pain felt and expressed by the wider family that day. It also took me some time to appreciate that the grief felt by our parents at the loss of a grandchild was compounded by watching their own children suffer.

In the time that followed Nathan's death, I went through the grieving process and did my best to care for Christopher who was just fourteen months old. It took me some time to appreciate how blessed I was that I had him to love and hold. People didn't seem to know the right things to say to us and many times I heard the phrase, "At least you still have Christopher." The words were well-meant and came from a desire to encourage, but instead they added to the pain. It suggested to me that as I already had a child, my second son's loss was of no lasting consequence as far as others were concerned.

Phil had his own personal struggles and, as the sole wage earner, needed to return to work. He showed remarkable strength and courage as a father and husband, for which I will always be thankful.

As Phil returned to work and the pattern of daily life filtered rudely back into our world, I was afraid of being alone with my grief and a demanding toddler. Neither of us felt ready to cope with the demands of normal life. I didn't want to put our son's loss behind me and forget. I wanted to be with Phil. Although realistically I knew he had to work to keep us, it seemed wrong that he should go out each day. It was as if I wanted to gather us all together and live in a protective bubble. I went through a myriad of emotions at that time, including anger and numbness. I also feared that I would forget my baby if I didn't keep thinking about him. Sometimes I felt panic that I had forgotten what he looked like or the couple of days we had had together.

The loss of our baby son felt so wrong and against the natural order of life. Children were meant to outlive their parents. Parents were not meant to bury their children. It felt like the future had been stolen from us, our dreams smashed. We would never know the person our son was to grow up to be, and that was the most painful thing of all, the thing I still wonder about, even now. There were no happy memories of time spent together before he left us, and just one snapshot photo of him.

I lived those early days in what felt like a kind of trance. However, we had amazing pastoral care from Peter and Mary Cook, who lovingly comforted and cared for us. They had also helped with the daunting task of arranging our son's funeral. I will be forever thankful for having had such an amazing, loving couple so close to us, caring for us in practical and spiritual ways during this time and beyond. We also had a lot of love and practical support from our extended family, in particular Phil's parents who had cared for Christopher throughout my time in hospital and until I was properly back on my feet after the funeral.

A few months later we had an appointment at the hospital with the consultant obstetrician to discuss Nathan's death. He told us that a percentage of mothers get pre-eclampsia in their first pregnancy and that it was rare I should have had it again in my second. It was virtually unheard of in subsequent pregnancies and so his advice to us was to go ahead and have another baby when we were ready.

CHAPTER THREE

Kerrie Louise Collins

Some months later, I found out I was pregnant again, with a due date in September. After the first three months, I was advised to rest, and with Christopher a lively twenty months, it was decided that we should move in with Phil's parents. Ann and Roy were delighted for us to do so and unselfishly gave up their home and time to help us. I had been told that lying on my left side was good for the baby and I followed all the advice I had been given. Ann devoted herself to looking after Christopher and me during those days; she spoilt me by cooking our favourite dinners and allowing me to rest, often waiting on me as I lay on the bed upstairs. However, despite being cared for so lovingly by family, I didn't feel settled. As the weeks progressed, I was aware that this baby was even less active than the last and I began to worry.

On the May Day bank holiday weekend, when I was about twenty weeks into my pregnancy, we called a local G.P. because I had felt virtually no movement from the baby for twenty-four hours. He said that he was unable to hear the foetal heartbeat and wanted to call an ambulance to take me to hospital. However, I was already feeling highly anxious and could not cope with (what seemed to me) the drama of an ambulance and so we made our own way to the hospital by car.

Filled with anxiety, we waited as a nurse placed a microphone to my abdomen to establish whether there was a heartbeat. To our immense and immediate relief, the familiar pattern of a heartbeat sounded clearly from the apparatus. Thank God, our baby was alive! The hospital staff still needed to connect me to a proper monitoring machine and so we waited until one became available. Due to my history and the heartbeat tracing the monitor produced, I was told to report to maternity outpatients weekly from this point on.

In the days that followed I felt increasingly unwell. We had no idea to what extent my symptoms were due to the stress we were experiencing or whether it was entirely the effect of the pregnancy on my body. I began experiencing migraine headaches for the first time ever, I had no energy and sometimes felt weak down one side of my body.

I am not certain whether I attended one or two of the weekly appointments, but it was not long before I became an inpatient once again. The obstetric team of doctors believed that there might be some underlying medical problem behind the issues in my pregnancies.

Once admitted, although on the maternity ward, I was seen primarily by the medical consultant. He became very interested in the rash I always seemed to have on my face, hands and arms during pregnancy. This had previously been dismissed as a pregnancy oestrogen rash, which is common and harmless. However, my rash was always present and turned much brighter when I was expecting. After a lot of deliberation, tests and research, the consultant decided that I had a condition known as Osler Weber Rendu Syndrome (more commonly known today as Hereditary Haemorrhagic Telangiectasia or H.H.T.). He advised me never to take aspirin or blood thinning medication due to the risk of bleeding. This created a problem for the obstetric doctors treating me because they had put me on aspirin to thin my blood and improve the blood flow through the placenta to the baby. However, in principle, my life took precedence and so the aspirin was stopped. I could not know what effect this might have on the outcome, but I believed that whatever the doctors did or didn't do, God was sovereign and could protect our baby.

My headaches and weakness were of primary concern following my diagnosis and so I underwent an urgent CT scan of my brain. This was done in order to identify any malformations of the veins and arteries in my head and to check for any bleeds. Such malformations are common in patients with H.H.T. and a brain haemorrhage had killed my maternal uncle and my great grandmother (although hers could have resulted from a fall). Once they had ruled out any serious problems there, the doctors sent me for some epilepsy type tests, with probes glued to my head, and then tested my 'bleeding time' by cutting me and timing how long it took for my blood to clot. Other checks were made on some of my other major organs.

The tests told them very little about what was going wrong and, as usual, my blood pressure increased and protein appeared in my urine. The baby was not growing normally and was relatively inactive with a slower than normal heart rate.

As the weeks went by, it transpired that the syndrome I had been diagnosed with was rarely seen and that most people remained undiagnosed until they had a major (often fatal) bleed, as both of my maternal uncles have done. As Kent and Canterbury was a teaching hospital, a write-up of my case had been posted somewhere in the hospital. Trainee doctors started asking if they could come in and see my rash. One day, the renal registrar came into my room and spent some time examining it. As I had suffered kidney failure after Nathan's delivery and had exhibited kidney symptoms during all three pregnancies, he seemed to think the rash was indicative of an underlying renal problem. As unbelievable as it seems to me now, he actually asked if he could return and take a very small sample of my skin to investigate. He never returned after that and I wondered whether my consultant had requested that he stay away until the baby was delivered.

It was the habit of the obstetric consultant, Mr Milligan (known as 'Spike' to the nursing staff), to pass by the door of my room of an evening on his way home and say goodnight. One evening, he came into my room on his way home. He said that he had a good friend and colleague in Guys Hospital called Kate Neals and that she had some specialist apparatus, called a Doppler scanner, which looked at and measured the blood flow through the placenta to the baby. She was attached to a specialist team there and Mr Milligan thought that I might benefit from seeing her. Immediately, I recognised the name as that of the registrar who had spotted Christopher's lack of growth and insisted on his early delivery, effectively saving his life.

Once we had arranged for my father-in-law to transport us up to London, we went from Canterbury Hospital to the specialist unit in Guys. It seemed strange that in hospital I was only allowed on my feet to visit the toilet and yet now I could make my own way to London! As it happened, Miss Neals was not there when we arrived and we were seen by one of her colleagues, a male Australian doctor. He performed the Doppler scan and also performed a procedure that had the potential to send me into early labour. I was only twenty-six weeks pregnant at the time. Using scanners to see the umbilical cord on the screen, he pushed a needle through my abdomen, into the womb, and took a blood sample from the cord. This was in order to measure the amount of oxygen the baby was getting, because the Doppler scan had shown very poor blood flow through the placenta. I was advised to keep perfectly still and I remember praying in my head and asking the Lord to protect our little baby girl whom we had already named Kerrie Louise. We had not wanted to know the gender of Christopher or Nathan before they were born, but when this pregnancy ran into problems, it helped me to be able to think of the baby more specifically.

We sat in an open-plan reception area for some time awaiting the results of the tests and, eventually, the doctor returned to speak to us. Instead of taking us into a less public area, he stopped where we were in the main antenatal reception area and (whilst chewing on his gum) said that he didn't "fancy this baby's chances". I was shocked and most upset by the way he had dealt with us, speaking of Kerrie's survival in such a casual and uncaring manner. We were asked to return in another two weeks for a repeat of the procedure.

Two weeks later, at twenty-eight weeks pregnant, we returned to Guys Hospital. This time, Miss Kate Neals was there and she performed the procedure. Fortunately, we did not encounter the doctor from the previous time. Had he been there, what we were about to go through would have become intolerable and I doubt I could have put up with his lack of empathy and unprofessional approach a second time.

As with the previous visit, we had to wait for the test results. However, this time Kate Neals took the utmost care in speaking with us and explaining all the potential outcomes of the tests to us beforehand in a small consultation room. We were given time to ask any questions and were afforded the privacy and comfort of the room whilst we waited for her to return with the results.

The doctor had gently explained that if the oxygen levels in the blood sample were good, I would go back to the ward at Canterbury and return to Guys for another scan in a week or so. If the oxygen levels were very poor, the baby would eventually die and would be stillborn. However, if the tests were in between, the baby would have to be delivered that day, either in London or back at Canterbury, in order for her to stand the best chance of survival.

It seemed like a very long time to wait and my prayer was simply that the oxygen was sufficient for Kerrie to have a chance of being born either that day or later.

Eventually Kate Neals returned. Kerrie needed to be delivered by C-section as soon as possible. We were given the option of staying at Guys or returning to Kent. We were familiar with the stresses and strains of having a premature baby in hospital and I was concerned that being in London would make visiting strenuous for Phil. So the decision was made to return to Kent. The doctor phoned my consultant there and we were told that a team would be ready to deliver Kerrie when I got back.

Although at that time twenty-eight weeks was the recognised gestation period that babies could survive if born prematurely, this baby was not the size of a normal twenty-eight-week-old. I was well aware that my little girl was weak, small and had already been fighting for her life a long time due to the restricted blood flow through the placenta and reduced amount of available oxygen. I was terrified she was too small and wouldn't make it. As we journeyed back towards Kent in the car, my mind drifted back to Nathan. Surely things would be OK this time. I dragged my thoughts back into the present, fought away the tears and fear, and prayed with all my heart that she would be OK; that she would survive.

Later that evening, Kerrie Louise was born. She weighed just 1 lb 2 ozs and was rushed straight from the operating theatre to the SCBU. She was put into a full incubator and ventilated because she was too small and weak to breathe for herself or to maintain her own body temperature. She was attached to a multitude of devices, tubes and wires to keep her alive. As with Nathan, they had carried out the C-section delivery whilst I was under general anaesthetic and I was therefore unable to see Kerrie for some time.

The day after surgery I was not well and kept vomiting. The doctor prescribed an additional drip to keep me hydrated until I was able to take fluids and keep them down. I was given a snapshot of my baby, which was placed by the bed.

Owing to the short time we had spent with Nathan, and my natural fears for this baby, I was very keen to get to SCBU as soon as possible to see her. Even though I was still feeling quite unwell, there was nothing on earth that was going to stop me from seeing my little girl and spending as many moments with her as I could. I persuaded the nurse to get me into a wheelchair and up to SCBU. I had always regretted the limited time I'd had with Nathan and the fact that we never took any photos, unaware that he was so sick. All we had to remember him by was the one instant snap taken by the staff for me.

As the nurse pushed me through the door of my room and into the corridor, the registrar who had examined me earlier that day started walking towards me. He had an expression on his face that suggested I shouldn't have left my room so soon. I don't remember what he said, but I announced to him that I was going to visit my baby and continued on my way. I think the edge of fortitude and certainty in my voice was sufficient to deter any further enquiry!

One day whilst we were visiting Kerrie in SCBU, we were approached by a member of staff and told of a drug trial being run at the hospital. The trial was for an artificial surfactant to help with the lubrication, and hence function, of the lungs in premature babies. They thought it would be helpful to Kerrie, but they needed our consent to administer it. As Nathan's death was due to hyaline membrane disease, caused by the absence of natural surfactants, this really encouraged us. Whilst pregnant in hospital, I had also received some steroid injections that had helped to mature Kerrie's lungs before the birth. At this point, we felt that she stood a much better chance of survival than her brother had done the previous year.

During the time Kerrie was in hospital, we prayed in faith for her healing and knew that many friends, family members and Christians from various churches were fervently praying for her to survive. However, although her lung function was good, her kidneys showed signs of failure from early on, and she was producing hardly any urine. The doctors performed various tests and scans to determine the cause of the problem, but remained mystified as to why she had renal failure. The kidneys were properly formed for her age of development and she had no recognisable disease.

Premature babies are frequently given scans of their brains to check for bleeds, which are a common occurrence. Often bleeds are superficial and later on tend to manifest as learning type difficulties as opposed to being life threatening or severely disabling. However, when Kerrie was five days old, we were visited by the consultant paediatrician and gently told that our daughter had suffered a substantial and significant brain bleed. This was in addition to the ongoing renal condition.

As we had been praying in faith that God would heal Kerrie's kidneys, this was a devastating blow. The doctor asked us what we wanted to do. It was really hard to try and take on board what he was very gently saying. But neither Phil nor I wanted our little girl to suffer anymore. Rather than leave her to face a slow death on life-support, we made the decision with the doctor to take her off life-supporting treatment and let her go. Nevertheless, we continued to pray fervently that God would heal her and others joined with us in this as they received news of her condition. We knew at this point that only a divine miracle could enable Kerrie to survive and our faith was strong that God could and might do so.

Once we had decided to stop treatment and everything was removed from Kerrie other than the ventilator, we were asked if there was anything they could do for us or Kerrie. We requested a hand and foot print and asked if she could be dressed. Until then she had looked like a little scrap of humanity, naked and covered in medical paraphernalia. I wanted her to look like a baby; our baby, our cherished little girl.

We returned to see Kerrie later and found her wearing a dress and looking peaceful for the first time. She had a ventilator tube going into her mouth, but was otherwise free from any medical equipment. As we took in the dress, we looked at each other in wonder. The dress was handmade and the material was covered in a pattern of doves carrying olive branches, which instantly reminded both of us of the story of Noah from the Bible. We were without doubt that God was saying something to us; that this was significant in some way.

Back in my room, we read the scriptures about Noah from the book of Genesis, chapter 8, verses 8 to 11:

> *"Then he sent out a dove to see if the water had receded from the surface of the ground. But the dove could find no place to set its feet because there was water over all the surface of the earth; so it returned to Noah in the ark. He reached out his hand and took the dove and brought it back to himself in the ark. He waited seven more days and again sent out the dove from the ark. When the dove returned to him in the evening, there in its beak was a freshly plucked*

olive leaf! Then Noah knew that the water had receded from the earth."

We attempted to make sense of the connection between Noah's story and our own situation and both understood the significance of the dove in the same way. Our interpretation was that Nathan represented the first flight of the dove. In Noah's story, he "reached out his hand and took the dove and brought it back to himself in the ark". God had taken Nathan back to be with Him in Heaven. Kerrie represented the second dove, which returned with an olive leaf proving there was life on the earth. We believed this meant that Kerrie would live and prayed in faith that God would raise her up.

Eventually, the appointed time came for staff to take our tiny daughter off the ventilator and hand her to us for the last time. They had arranged for this to take place at a time when the unit was not overly busy with visitors and this time everything was done with the utmost care and compassion for us as a family. A screen was put around Kerrie's incubator, the doctor removed the ventilator and then she was handed to a nurse who walked with us to the small bedroom on the unit. Kerrie was handed over to us and, despite being off the ventilator, she was alive.

I was filled with conflicting emotions and my heart raced inside my chest. Was this it? Were we about to see a spectacular modern-day miracle? Our faith was strong, but at the same time my heart felt overwhelmingly sad and tears flowed freely and unbidden down my face. After a short while, Kerrie took her last breath and, having checked her, the doctor confirmed there was no pulse. Yet even now there was hope that God would raise her up for us and give us the miracle we had asked for. We waited...

Eventually, truth dawned like a threatening tsunami bearing down on us. It struck with full force, engulfing us in its hideous depth and we realised Kerrie was gone. She was just five days old.

Once again we faced the agony of leaving the hospital foyer with empty arms, only this time it was on the day our daughter had passed away. There are no words to describe the feelings we experienced.

Having left the hospital, we drove straight to our home. We went into our son Christopher's bedroom, sat on the bed together and wept bitterly, clinging to each other. It felt like we would never be able to stop, like our world was ending. I became afraid of the depth and strength of our grief and told Phil I couldn't cope. He had always been like a rock to me, able to deal with anything. I began to panic and felt as if I was unable to breathe. Caught in a selfish survival mode, I asked him to stop. Phil's interpretation of this was that his permission to grieve was being taken away from him and, sadly, his response was to repress some of his feelings.

We dried our tears and, as we had already spoken to our pastor, we then drove to his home. We stayed there overnight where he and Mary cared for and comforted us. The next morning our G.P. (having been contacted by the hospital) visited us there to check how we were. He told us not to give up on having another child. It seemed such an odd thing to say given the circumstances and the timing.

The following day we headed back to Phil's parents' house, where we had been living whilst Kerrie was in hospital. This was the first time we had seen them since her death and it must have been difficult for them. They had their own grief to deal with and yet were needed to care for us and Christopher.

We came into the house and it was as if nothing had happened. We were offered a cup a tea and we all sat down in the lounge. Conversation started about general things and as I sat there with the mug of tea in my hands, a raging tide of emotion bubbled up within me. Our baby daughter had just died and I couldn't stand that everyone was seemingly acting as if nothing was wrong. I stood as little chance of containing the powerful feelings welling up in me as I would attempting to stop a volcanic eruption, and after a few minutes of trying, I exploded and the mug flew out of my hands. I ran from the room, hot tears streaming down my face and Phil and his parents swiftly followed. Phil's parents embraced the pair of us and said that they hadn't known how to deal with the situation. We were all in tears as they expressed to us their sadness over Kerrie's and Nathan's deaths.

CHAPTER FOUR

The Battle

We stayed with Phil's parents until after Kerrie's funeral and then moved back home. Phil had to return to work again and I had to continue caring for our lively two-year-old who had no understanding of what had happened or why Mummy was so sad. I felt overwhelmed by my loss and wasn't able to cope with the demands of getting back to 'normal'. As before, Phil switched to 'work mode' and with courage and fortitude continued with daily life. I was unaware of what was really going on inside him or that he now felt unable to express his real feelings. I have a hazy memory of challenging him as to how he could just seemingly switch off and carry on. The truth was he believed that was what he had to do. He never mentioned the things I said shortly after Kerrie's death and so I was unable to put it right. From the time I first met Phil, I had suffered with a tendency to depression and he took on a protective role.

After Nathan's death, I had recovered well mentally and physically, and following the obstetric consultant's comments on the post mortem, I had been hopeful that we would have another baby. This time there was no such hope and this, along with the double loss in just eleven months, left me feeling as if I had fallen into a big black hole.

A couple of weeks after we had returned home I was still experiencing very heavy bleeding, so my G.P. sent me to the hospital where I was readmitted due to concern that there may be an infection. I underwent a minor surgical procedure to clean the inside of the uterus.

Unfortunately, even then hospital beds were at a premium and I was put in the gynaecological ward opposite a mother having a termination. This seemed so wrong and I found the situation difficult to cope with.

31

Fortunately, I was only on the ward for one night and was then able to return home.

As the weeks went by, I found that I was unable to speak to God in prayer anymore and I was aware of a black ball of anger growing inside of me. Why? Why? Why? Why hadn't God healed my daughter? Why had He allowed both babies to die? What hadn't we learnt through the first loss that meant we had to experience another? Why us? Others in church had healthy babies. What had I done wrong? Was God punishing us?

I became very depressed and the woman who visited me from a baby bereavement group[1] was concerned for my mental well-being. I had constant panic attacks. I found it increasingly difficult to go out and couldn't bear to be in the car. If I had a panic attack in the car, Phil would have to stop so I could get out.

A short while after my admission to hospital to have my womb cleaned, I was admitted yet again because of pain in my chest. I had some nuclear investigations of my lungs and was discharged after a few days. I later discovered that I had had a lung clot.

Whilst I was in hospital the second time my pastor visited me. He lovingly challenged me to talk to him about my feelings. He wanted to know what was wrong and how he could help. I knew the answer to his question but felt ashamed of my thoughts and feelings towards God and therefore was unable to enter into a dialogue with anyone about it. I think he probably had a good idea as to the nature of the problem, but unless I was brave enough to open up to him, he was unable to help me. However, the challenge did stir something in me and eventually I realised that I was not going to get better until I faced up to the issue and dealt with it.

The anger and misery that I had kept bottled up inside had been slowly destroying everything in my life. All joy and peace had ebbed

---

[1] This was a "Sands" group. "Sands" is a stillborn and neonatal death charity who support bereaved parents and grandparents.
Website: *www.sands.org.uk/support*
Email: *helpline@uk.sands.org*
Phone: 020-74365881
Another helpful Christian charity is "Care for the Family". They support parents of children with special needs, besides helping families with other challenging circumstances.
Website: *www.careforthefamily.org.uk*

away leaving me at rock bottom. Although I continued to attend church on a regular basis, I was just going through the motions and doing what I believed to be right. I had not really been able to pray or worship since Kerrie's death.

Then one day, when I felt I could go on no longer, I found the courage to approach God and open up to Him. I waited until I was alone and Chris was having a nap upstairs. I took the phone off the hook, shut the sitting room door, sat down and closed my eyes. I felt deep shame and guilt about my feelings as I approached God. I knew that before I spoke a word to Him, He already knew what was in my heart. I wasn't about to tell Him something He was unaware of, but until I was honest with Him about it, there was a barrier in our relationship. I knew that the barrier had been erected on my side and that I was the one who needed to break it down.

I began the conversation quietly in tears, telling Him that I couldn't go on; but as I opened up my heart, the anger and bitterness that had been so carefully contained burst forth uncontrollably like puss from an infected wound. I found myself railing at, and questioning, the Almighty as to why He had taken my babies away from me. Hot angry tears streamed down my face and my body shook with the depth of emotion and sobs rising from deep within me.

Finally, when all the poison was out and there was nothing left to say, I sat exhausted on the floor with my head on the sofa in silence. However, to my amazement, it wasn't a bad silence, but one that felt strangely peaceful. There was no defence or any words of rebuke for my accusations towards Him; just peace and an immense feeling of being loved and understood. I remained in the same position for some time with my eyes closed, and it felt as if my head was resting in the lap of a loving parent and that I was (at last) being comforted in my inmost being.

From that day, He began to heal my heart and I learned to come to terms with one of the most important aspects of God. He is Sovereign and doesn't need to justify His actions. I was able to accept what He had chosen to do and concede that even if I didn't understand, it was somehow for the best because He is a good God. As I write now, I am able to revisit the scripture from the night before Nathan's birth in Psalm 139, in particular verse 16: "Your eyes saw my unformed body. All the days ordained for me were written in Your book before one of them came to be." The Lord God had always planned that Nathan and

Kerrie would spend a short time on this Earth. It was no failure or slip up on His part, but rather a planned part of our journey with Him. We will be reunited with them in Heaven.

Another facet of God I also experienced at that time is that He is not like my earthly father; so quick to mete out punishment even when I was innocent of any wrongdoing. My Heavenly Father is slow to anger and abounding in love (Psalm 103, verse 8). I had been angry at Him, but when I asked His forgiveness, He gave it unconditionally along with His love. The panic attacks gradually stopped and the depression lifted.

If I never know the reason God chose to take Nathan and Kerrie home so soon, I am content knowing that I grew much closer to the Lord as a result of all that happened to us. Before I went through these difficult times, I had been lazy with reading scriptures and relied heavily upon what I received in church on Sundays and at mid-week meetings. I was a passive Christian, a bit of a spectator, content to be fed by someone else doing the work, and was blessed to be in a church where the Word was very well preached. But all that changed in me and I developed a new passion for the Bible and reading it. I began to transfer a lot of head knowledge about God into heart experience, and my relationship with Christ flourished.

CHAPTER FIVE

From Adoption to Prophecy

A year after Kerrie's death, I became unwell with swollen painful joints and water problems, and was admitted to hospital. I was unable to bend my knees, which meant I couldn't get on the floor and play properly with Christopher. I was also extremely tired and spent a lot of time lying on my bed or sleeping. This led to several outpatient appointments with various consultants trying to pinpoint the cause. Eventually, I was put under the care of a rheumatologist who, after many blood tests and investigations, told me I had lupus (S.L.E.). Lupus is an autoimmune disorder where the immune system attacks healthy tissue in the body. It can attack virtually any system and can be life-threatening. I was put on steroids to treat the condition and four years later was finally able to function without them.

The cause of the poor blood flow through the placenta and my illness during pregnancy was, in fact, related to the lupus, in that I also had antiphospholipid syndrome (also known as Hughes syndrome), which is in the same group of autoimmune diseases. In antiphospholipid syndrome, the immune system attacks the blood, causing the platelets to be sticky, which can lead to blood clots. However, antiphospholipid syndrome was still being researched at the time and I was not properly diagnosed for fifteen years; eventually I was diagnosed by Professor Hughes himself after I had been told I had had two lung clots.

As it was clearly unwise for us to try and have another child naturally, and as we still desperately wanted a sibling for Christopher and another child to love, we made the decision to adopt a child.

We contacted social services and began the exhaustive process of becoming approved adopters for a baby girl aged 0-6 months. This

35

involved attending an adoption course over several months and receiving regular visits from an assigned social worker who scrutinised us both, particularly my childhood and dysfunctional family life during my formative years. At the end of the process, two years later, our application to adopt was taken to a panel.

Eventually, having been passed by the panel, we were put on the register and waited to be selected as adopters for a compatible baby. At this time, social services sought to place babies with people who were of the same ethnicity as the child, so that the child did not stand out as being obviously adopted.

During the two years we waited on the adoption register, I learnt to drive and got involved at Christopher's primary school listening to children read, which I found very rewarding. As we would need to be available quickly when the right baby was found for us, it was not possible to go back to work as such and so I filled my time volunteering in various ways. On one occasion I was asked to cover for a classroom assistant who looked after a boy in the reception class with Down's syndrome for two weeks while she recovered from surgery. I was later approached by the head teacher when a similar permanent position came up at the school. She knew that we were waiting to adopt a baby and when, on questioning me, she discovered that I might have to leave the post at short notice, she decided that this would be problematic. My fluctuating health also restricted me to a large extent until my condition was stabilised by treatment.

Being at home alone for quite a lot of the time meant that I sometimes felt lonely and, of course, broody. So we added our first pet to the family – a four-month-old kitten called McLeod. McLeod was a real delight and soon helped to fill the need in me to nurture a baby. I very much enjoyed having him around and watching him grow. I had prayed for him to be an affectionate cat and my prayers were more than answered. In fact, McLeod behaved for the entirety of his fourteen years as if he had been created for the sole purpose of being adored and fussed over!

A month later, there was a special healing meeting arranged at the Pentecostal church we attended. People were encouraged to come along to be anointed with oil and prayed over for God to heal them of any sickness. Phil and I both went along and I joined the queue of those awaiting prayer. I didn't set out for the meeting with any great expectation, but I did feel very close to God during the service and there was a strong sense of His presence among us.

Towards the end of the meeting, when most of those seeking to be healed had been prayed over, there was a time of musical worship and thanksgiving. During this time, a close friend came up to me and said that she had a message from God for us (a prophecy). She admitted that she was feeling very nervous about sharing it in case she had heard incorrectly or it had been of her own imagining. She had spoken to the leader of the meeting, seeking his guidance before approaching me. She told me that God had seen our faithfulness and that He was going to give us our hearts' desire. Our hearts' desire was to have a baby girl of our own. A couple of minutes later, she returned to me again and confessed that she had not given me the prophecy correctly due to her fear. She believed that God had told her that He *had* given us our hearts' desire. I was stunned and totally amazed that God had said this to us. I had come wanting to be healed of lupus and now my friend was saying God had given us a daughter. It was a lot to take on board.

As we left the meeting that night, I was tearful and felt overwhelmed by the many thoughts and emotions this message had created. It was exciting, but also very scary. Did we dare to believe the prophecy or not? We went home and discussed what had been said and aired our thoughts and fears with one another. Unless this was from God, we could be about to put ourselves in a difficult and dangerous place again.

A short time later, I had a positive pregnancy test. The baby was due in February the following year. There was much excitement and those who had been involved with the prophecy at the meeting formed a small support/prayer group for us. We received loving, faith-filled support from them and also from Peter and Mary. I was confident at the outset that as God had told us we would have "our hearts' desire", I would (for the first time) have a normal full-term pregnancy and a healthy baby girl at the end.

CHAPTER SIX

Katelyn Louise Collins

A s usual, the first three months went well, with only nausea and morning sickness to cope with. I felt happy and confident that all would be well. I was particularly encouraged once the first scan confirmed that this baby was indeed a girl!

Due to my medical history, the pregnancy was considered high risk and I was therefore seen early and regularly. By now there was a Doppler scanner and other specialist equipment at the Kent and Canterbury hospital and Kate Neals, having moved back from Guys Hospital, was the specialist consultant dealing with problem or high-risk pregnancies. However, because I believed this pregnancy was a promise and gift from God, I also believed that nothing would go wrong this time and that all scans and precautions would prove unnecessary.

Once I was into the second trimester, the Doppler scans began to show that this baby, like her siblings before her, was not getting a good flow of blood from the placenta. She was also showing signs of poor growth and was smaller than expected for the stage of the pregnancy. This stunned us and I felt afraid for the first time. However, we were determined to trust God and so we prayed. As soon as we told others about the results of the Doppler scans, those who had been supporting us visited us together and prayed over the baby and me. As they prayed fervently and with faith, they declared God's prophetic promise to us and thanked Him for the life within me. They shared scriptures on God's faithfulness and encouraged us.

In my human frailty it was very hard to hold on to the promise of God when all the evidence pointed to a re-run of my earlier pregnancies with an even smaller, weaker baby. Each pregnancy I had been through, the baby had been more severely growth-retarded and delivered earlier. Christopher was born at thirty-seven weeks at 3 lbs 12 ozs; Nathan John, thirty-one weeks at 2 lbs 5 ozs; Kerrie Louise at twenty-eight weeks and 1 lb 2 ozs. However, in spite of all the evidence against a good outcome, God continued to speak to us, quieten our troubled hearts and build our faith to believe Him. Different scriptures came up in daily readings to encourage us when we doubted. During this time, we went on holiday to Somerset and visited a local church on the Sunday. Even there, we found God speaking to us through the preaching and scripture without anyone knowing us or what we were going through. I wrote all the encouraging words in a little notebook and kept it in my bible. When I was feeling down or began to doubt, I took out the book and read through the things recorded there.

In the previous pregnancies, I had been admitted to hospital because I was ill. Typically, I would have high blood pressure, swollen ankles and a lot of protein in my urine. This time, I continued to be well and at home. Owing to the diagnosis of lupus a few years before, the consultant had decided to put me onto a small dose of oral steroid to treat me and a small dose of soluble aspirin to hopefully thin the blood to aid its transit through the placenta to the baby. The steroid she chose had been successful in treating the symptoms of the lupus when it had first flared up and it was successful in keeping me well in this pregnancy. However, nothing seemed to improve the blood flow and rate of growth for this baby and each week when she scanned me, the consultant became less hopeful of a live outcome.

At twenty-five weeks of the pregnancy Kate Neals took us into a small room following the scan and spoke to us about the continuing lack of growth and poor blood flow. She expressed her regret that treatment had not been successful for the baby and her concern that by the following week the scan would reveal the baby had perished.

As we walked back to the car following our talk with the doctor, we discovered that neither of us felt affected by what she had said and that we both felt a certainty that she was wrong. We gathered people around us to pray again. By now, there were various churches in England and other countries praying for our baby.

We returned for the following week's scan in faith and were told that not only was she still alive but that there had been an improvement in the blood flow and a "tad" of growth. God really encouraged us with that and we praised Him and thanked Him; but there was still a very long and hard road ahead.

Another remarkable encouragement from God around this time was the revelation of why our first daughter, Kerrie Louise, had been wearing a dress covered in doves with olive branches in their beaks. This revelation was to give us the hope and faith to carry us through the weeks and months ahead and remains the single most definitive thing that God has ever spoken to us. To ensure we were in absolutely no doubt whatsoever this was a divine revelation, God revealed the same thing to both Phil and me whilst he was at work and I was reading the Bible at home.

I went to the book of Genesis in the Bible and again read the account of Noah and how he determined there was dry land by sending out a dove and a raven. Genesis 8 tells that Noah first sent out a raven and it kept flying back and forth until the water had dried up from the earth. It did not return to the ark. This represented our son Christopher, who survived. Then Noah sent out a dove and it returned to the ark because there was nowhere to set its feet. This represented our son Nathan, for whom God reached out His hand and brought him back to Himself. Seven days later Noah sent the dove out again and when it returned to him it had in its beak a freshly plucked olive leaf. This represented our first daughter, Kerrie Louise, who was dressed in doves with olive branches and who returned to Him. Noah waited seven more days and sent the dove out again, "…but this time it did not return to him." This was to represent our second, unborn daughter, Katelyn Louise, who would remain on the earth. I cannot remember whether I phoned Phil first or he phoned me, but the same thing occurred to us simultaneously. When we had tried to work out the meaning of the dress when Kerrie was dying, we had not counted the raven in the story and saw Kerrie as the child who would remain on the earth. Now came God's clear revelation that the dress was a promise of a baby to come later, who would not die.

When the doctor saw an improvement at twenty-six weeks, she decided I should be admitted to hospital the following week with a plan to deliver Katelyn at twenty-seven to twenty-eight weeks. I was admitted on the Thursday but, over the weekend, the registrar who was caring for me began to panic about remaining spaces in the SCBU and, with triplets being delivered early, thought he needed to transfer me. He arranged for me to be moved on the Monday. This was upsetting and worrying, but we prayed and left it in God's hands. On Monday morning Kate Neals came straight down into the side ward where I was and simply stated that under no circumstances would I be moving anywhere and that I would most definitely be having my baby there! She seemed a little rattled, to say the least, and I suspect that her registrar fully felt her displeasure at his actions in her absence.

On November 30th, our little girl, Katelyn Louise, was delivered by C-section under epidural anaesthetic and weighed just 1 lb (the smallest surviving delivery at the Kent and Canterbury Hospital). Knowing that our baby was going to weigh around a pound and be ventilated, I asked God if He would allow me to hear her cry before she was taken to SCBU. I had never heard Nathan or Kerrie cry because I had been unconscious when they were delivered and then they were in special care. Once a ventilator tube is inserted, and babies are sedated, they don't make any noise.

Dr Long was the paediatrician on duty in theatre to take our daughter when she was born. He was expecting a weak, limp little scrap of life needing immediate intervention and ventilation to help her to breathe. However, he was handed a screaming, kicking miniature baby, which totally bemused and delighted him. He said he didn't know what to do with her; that he hadn't expected her to be breathing so well. He allowed her to continue breathing on her own until she showed signs that she might become exhausted and he then made the decision to ventilate her. She was placed in an incubator in SCBU, the unit that became her home for the next three months. When he first spoke to us about her, he said that, based on his experience and statistics, she had only an even (fifty-fifty) chance of survival at that point.

Within the first few days of her life, it was clear that our daughter still had a real fight on her hands to win the battle for survival. We held on tightly to the promise of God in our spirits and minds, but we are human and the early weeks felt as though we had taken a ride on an emotional rollercoaster and we were thrown around relentlessly. One minute glimmers of hope and joy, the next watching a life-threatening crisis rise up and hold our helpless little girl in its cruel grip.

The first crisis for Katelyn began as I was still under the influence of strong medication and recovering from surgery. Something had happened whilst the doctors were trying to establish a line (needle with a tube) in her umbilicus and she was bleeding. This was quickly dealt with and a blood transfusion given. When I first saw her in SCBU, she already looked sick and wounded. Her belly button had been stitched where the bleed had been and she had stitches in the side of her head. On enquiring, I discovered that her head had been cut, just above her ear, during the delivery. Again, I was aware of God's grace upon her as I realised how close it was to her face.

I was amazed at how doctors had managed to put tubes into various veins to provide her with the medicines she needed. She was the size of about half a bag of sugar and the palm of her hand the size of my thumbnail, her head the size of a small peach. Phil's dad wanted other members of the family who had not yet seen her to be able to gauge her size and took a picture of her next to a king-size Mars bar; it was about the same length. I praised God for the skill and gifting of these doctors and nurses to be able to take care of such tiny human beings.

It was tough, but all the way along God continued to encourage us and give us the strength we needed each day. A few weeks before Katelyn had been born, another baby weighing a couple of ounces more had been admitted to SCBU. We chatted to her parents and we supported one another. We were given some of their daughter's tiny dresses for Katelyn to wear whilst she was in an incubator.

———————————————

All babies, whether born prematurely or at full term, need to pass the plug of meconium from their bowels and this usually occurs within the first couple of days. When this failed to happen for Katelyn and her abdomen began swelling, there was concern that she had an obstruction in her bowels, which, in the worst case, could lead to gangrene (the bowel dying and rotting). We passed the message about this crisis around the various groups of people who were praying for her. When we next contacted the ward, the ward sister was thrilled to tell us what had happened. She had placed apparatus on the incubator and was literally about to start an irrigation process to see if the blockage could be washed out, when Katelyn suddenly passed the meconium herself. This was incredibly good news because it spared Katelyn an intrusive procedure or even surgery. She was still very tiny and either could have had dire consequences at this stage. God had answered our prayer.

There were many difficult times whilst Katelyn was in intensive care, but perhaps the most traumatic event happened right in front of us one Sunday afternoon when she was a few weeks old. Although tiny, Katelyn needed very little oxygen or pressure from the ventilator at this time. It was only due to her lack of energy to sustain her own breathing that she was initially ventilated. On this particular day, Katelyn had pulled her tube out (quite a common occurrence in SCBU). She was breathing well on her own and so a decision was made to let her continue. When we phoned after church, the nurse reported that she was off the ventilator. We borrowed Phil's dad's video camera and set off to celebrate this exciting step towards her recovery.

When we arrived at the unit, we went through the usual procedure of handwashing, etc., and then went into the intensive care room. As we entered, Katelyn had suffered a respiratory arrest and the team were trying to resuscitate her. Our arrival made working on their tiny patient even more difficult and so we were ushered out to wait. As her life literally hung in the balance, all I could do was offer up silent prayers to the Lord that He would intervene in this situation and that she would be OK. Memories of the night Nathan had died flooded my mind but I held on once again to God's promise that I would have my heart's desire.

After what seemed like a long wait, but was probably just a few minutes, the consultant paediatrician came to let us know that Katelyn was back on the ventilator and was fine. He explained how difficult it had been to make the decision when to take her off the ventilator due to her extremely small size for her gestation. He explained that it was always best to get babies off ventilation as soon as possible due to the risk of lung infection and other complications. Before she left the intensive care room, Katelyn was to suffer lung infections and a collapsed lung.

During the first few weeks, babies in intensive care have their heads measured and their brains scanned to check for any bleeds on the brain. We were told from quite early on that Katelyn had sustained minor bleeds, which would probably lead to some "learning-type difficulties" later on. When faced with such a small, sick baby, these words can seem of little importance compared to the life-threatening crises that occur. For me there was also a relief there had not been any substantial bleeds, like those Kerrie had suffered, which would have resulted in more serious brain damage.

A couple of weeks after the respiratory arrest we walked onto the unit to find Katelyn not only off ventilation but moved into the high dependency part of the unit onto something called CPAP (a small amount of oxygen delivered via a tube under her nose). This was wonderful news and a cause for much thanksgiving to God. However, removal of the ventilator brought unwelcome issues for our tiny daughter. For the first four to five weeks of her life, she had been used to having something constantly in her mouth to suck. This also turned out to be an issue for the nursing staff, who now heard her lusty cry and spent much time stood at her side offering a finger for her to suck!

Progress was rapid from this point on and within just three days, Katelyn went onto the ordinary part of the ward where she needed much less medical intervention and the focus was on her gaining weight. She was still tiny, weighing in at just a kilo (2 lbs 2 ozs) at this point. Unfortunately, her unusual size for a baby in the ordinary nursery led to occasional mistakes, the most memorable for me being her first real bath.

Babies on this part of the ward were bathed as routine and one day the nurse assigned to her care asked if I would like to help bath Katelyn. We undressed her and a funnelled tube providing some oxygen was placed near her face as we lowered her into the water. The ward sister happened to walk into this area and past us at that moment and immediately pointed out to the nurse that, unlike other babies on the ward, Katelyn was too small and in need of keeping warm to be fully undressed and placed in a bath. It was an unfortunate error for the nurse to have made and she was most upset and apologetic. There had never been such a tiny baby on this part of the ward before and she had not realised that normal routine should not be applied to this patient. We hastily dried and dressed Katelyn again and placed her back into the special, heated cot. It was similar to an incubator, but had no lid, so the baby was kept warm and any equipment, tubes and wires were easily accommodated. Katelyn soon warmed up again and no harm was done, but she didn't have any further baths until she had gained more weight.

On January 23rd, Katelyn came out of an incubator and into a heated cot, and two days after that she was in an ordinary cot. She now weighed 2 lbs 6 ozs.

In February, when Katelyn had put on a lot of weight, was demand-feeding from me and a bottle, and was progressing towards a date to come home, there was an outbreak of a virus on the ward. To normal healthy adults, it was a particularly nasty, feverish cold; but to these vulnerable little babies it posed a real threat. One by one, we watched as the babies all seemed to go down with it, aggravating any breathing problems or hitting any weaknesses they had. From doing well and beginning to look like a regular (albeit small) baby, our daughter went down with the virus on February 12th and suddenly looked like she was struggling again. We came onto the ward one day to discover she needed a blood transfusion as a result of the virus. Doctors had experienced difficulty putting in a line for the blood and therefore had to resort to inserting a needle into the soft part of her head. She looked terrible and I remember being very upset by a jovial comment from a nurse. They had taped a tiny plastic dish to her head to protect the line from being pulled out. The nurse could see I was concerned and attempted to make light of the situation by saying Katelyn was wearing her party hat for us. We had been through months of emotional strain by then and I was just too drained to see the humour at the time.

Eventually, on February 26th, close to her original due date and still weighing just 4 lbs, Katelyn was discharged and allowed to come home. It was a very special day of celebration and we invited the local press to be there. This was in order to give the unit publicity and hopefully some charitable donations to its funds.

CHAPTER SEVEN

Mountains Made Low

We had seen a number of other babies leave the ward in the time we had been there and it didn't escape our notice that although our daughter was the smallest surviving baby the unit had ever seen, she was going home healthy and without oxygen. Several premature babies, including the one who weighed a few ounces more, went home with CPAP oxygen.

On being discharged from the hospital, we were asked whether we wanted to take a sleep apnoea alarm home with us. Like many premature babies, Katelyn would sometimes forget to breathe and had been attached to a monitor throughout her time on the ward to check this. Having the alarm at home would alert us to this missed breath and give us the opportunity to tickle her feet, causing her to gasp if she didn't do so herself.

It was a tough decision, which we talked about and weighed up. We were concerned that if we took the device home, we would always lack confidence and become dependent on it. We wanted to trust God and, given all He had already done for her, we decided not to take it home. The hospital was entirely happy about this. We would not have done so against their advice.

I would like to say that when Katelyn arrived home all was perfect and plain-sailing. However, three months in a medical environment was bound to have had some influence on how she settled. The early months with Katelyn were not easy! Still being tiny, she required feeding every three hours. I was partially breastfeeding alongside a bottle of special high-calorie formula at every feed. After the months of stress leading up to her homecoming, I was already tired, but this quickly turned to feeling exhausted. In addition to frequent feeds around the clock, Katelyn was also very unsettled and used to scream for hours every day (particularly in the early evening, onwards).

I was also unsettled by the experience of having Katelyn home. She was exactly the same weight Christopher had been when he came home, but he had not been as poorly beforehand. At first, we kept the baby next to our bed in a crib, just as we had done with our firstborn. However, I found it difficult to sleep and so we moved her to the adjacent bedroom and placed a baby alarm by our bed. I frequently panicked when there was too long a gap between her breaths and missed out on a lot of sleep. This meant that when she did wake for a change and feed, I was exhausted. Gradually I learned to put Katelyn in God's care for the night and rest in peace.

As I returned to the outpatient clinic to see the paediatrician with Katelyn over the following year, it became increasingly clear to me just how God had blessed us concerning her health. Often, I would see familiar faces from the ward and their babies would have obvious physical/mental disabilities or still be on oxygen. It affected me greatly to sit in the clinic with them and I would often come home and fervently pray over those babies, as well as praising God for all He had done.

Throughout her childhood, Katelyn has faced many things that could have caused her to fail at school or resulted in long-term physical problems. I believe totally in the power of praying parents, and Phil and I prayed throughout her childhood that God would give our daughter what she needed to overcome her difficulties as well as praying more specific prayers as situations arose. It became clear as her personality developed that He had partially answered this by gifting her with a determined and tenacious attitude to life. We also saw God move in many other ways and He always seemed to bring her through the difficulties that lay before her.

Whilst in hospital, premature babies are thoroughly checked for all the known physical problems that can occur. Katelyn had numerous checks on her eyes, a hearing test, plus brain scans, X-rays and regular visits from a physiotherapist.

Other than the minor brain bleeds, which we were advised would cause some learning difficulties, our daughter was diagnosed with a squint in both eyes and also needed regular visits from the physiotherapist at home to correct her posture (thus enabling her to sit, crawl and then walk). Owing to the fact that small babies have lots of space in the womb, they do not draw their limbs into a curled position and therefore can lack the ability to bring their limbs round like other babies do. However, in spite of this problem, by seventeen months (fourteen months from her due birth date), Katelyn took her first steps.

We were amazed by how little effect the squint had on Katelyn. She attended the hospital regularly for some years to have it checked in case a surgical intervention was required to correct it before it caused a serious problem with her vision. However, to the unprofessional observer, including me, it was very difficult to spot her eyes turning outwards. When I queried this during one appointment, I was told that this was because Katelyn corrected the squint so well herself. She continued to do so and was eventually discharged. There have been no problems whatsoever from the condition.

Although Katelyn had a very healthy childhood and the physical effects of her premature start were minor, she has had to contend with the problems resulting from her brain bleeds. There were developmental issues, particularly with her gross motor movements, fine motor skills and understanding of language and speech. In the early years a paediatrician saw her regularly and she attended a specialist preschool in Sittingbourne where she had one-to-one help and regular speech therapy.

The early years were especially difficult for Katelyn and me, as she had undiagnosed Asperger syndrome, in addition to language problems, making it almost impossible for her to communicate her fears until they reached a level of distress she was unable to contain. Even something as ordinary as a trip to the supermarket was upsetting for her as she was overwhelmed by the noise and crowded space around her. She would scream all the way round and I would encounter frowns and comments from others who judged me an incompetent parent. Eventually, on the advice of the health visitor, I stopped taking her with me. It has forever changed my attitude to screaming children in public places. It's so easy to judge when you don't know what's going on.

At age five, Katelyn was referred to child physio/occupational therapy by a specialist health visitor. She was later diagnosed with dyspraxia and a severe auditory memory problem. She attended summer school workshops for a couple of years to work on her gross and fine motor skills and had some weekly after school classes in Canterbury to help with her handwriting. On one of her visits to our home, the health visitor listened to my concerns about Katelyn's rigid routines and other behaviours, which I had not seen in Christopher. She advised me that Katelyn had Asperger's tendencies, but not Asperger's itself. She said that she saw many babies and young children who had been premature, like our daughter, and that a number of things, including the Asperger's tendencies, were common. For this reason, I never took her for a proper assessment until she requested it herself at seventeen, and was formally diagnosed as having mild autism.

Perhaps the biggest emotional difficulties for Katelyn, and for us as her parents, have been caused by her autism. She was bullied throughout her primary school years, as well as at secondary school. Most of it would be considered as mild, in that no serious physical harm came to her. However, had she not had a secure home life and a loving Heavenly Father, I believe that the rejection and persecution for being 'different' could have broken her. I found it particularly upsetting because I had also been bullied as a child, both by my father at home and by a boy at school, so I knew the pain she was suffering. I felt a deep sense of being helpless to help my child and anger at those causing her pain. It was a real battle, in which I often felt heartbroken, but I continued to pour love into the wounds and pray God's healing and protection over her. I now see before me a strong young woman of twenty, whom God has allowed to go through these trials to shape and mould her into the incredible person she is. She is kind, caring, gentle, loving and has a level of empathy rarely seen in those with autism.

There is a scripture in the Bible, in Isaiah 40, verses 4 to 5, which says:

> *"Every valley shall be raised up, every mountain and hill made low; the rough ground shall become level, the rugged places a plain. And the glory of the Lord will be revealed."*

I believe that this scripture describes the work that God has done in Katelyn's life in bringing her to the place she is in now.

The paediatrician from Medway who saw Katelyn on a regular basis until she was five predicted (based on her experience with children like Katelyn with brain injuries) that the learning difficulties would begin to be really noticeable from about the age of seven, when she could lag way behind her peers. This didn't happen. She had some difficulty with numeracy and with spelling, which resulted in some additional small group work, but she worked hard and left primary school with an average attainment in English and slightly below average attainment in Maths. Katelyn went on to attend the local secondary school and within the first year began to show sudden and significant improvement in her ability at Maths. This improvement continued and she passed a GCSE exam at grade C.

Throughout her primary school years, I suspected Katelyn had dyslexia and spoke with the British Dyslexic Association, who sent me a pack on what to look for. The school did some screening tests and told me they had only picked up a specific spelling problem. When Katelyn again struggled in secondary school, I spoke with the Special Educational Needs Co-ordinator and she offered to run some tests. These showed Katelyn to be at high risk and picked up thirteen indicators of dyslexia.

Throughout her secondary school journey, Katelyn's teachers commented that she was a very hard-working and diligent student. However, given that she has a severe auditory memory problem, dyslexia, dyspraxia and Asperger syndrome, I believe that hard work alone cannot explain Katelyn's level of attainment in her school career of fifteen GCSEs (including four A*s and an A) and then BTEC diplomas equivalent to two A-levels at grade A and two at grade C. I don't wish to take anything away from Katelyn and the remarkable, hard-working young woman she is, but I believe that, along with her hard work, the hand of God has helped lift her over many of the obstacles she has encountered throughout her young life.

When I think back to God's promise in May 1995 that He would give us our hearts' desire and I see my complete, healthy and grown-up family, I am filled with thanksgiving to the God of miracles. I have two beautiful and precious gifts of God and two more awaiting me in Heaven. The Lord God has given to me beauty instead of ashes, the oil of gladness instead of mourning and a garment of praise instead of a spirit of despair (from Isaiah 61, verse 3). All praise be to Him!

EPILOGUE

O ne Sunday, I felt compelled to give a spoken testimony as to God's goodness and faithfulness in the life of my daughter Katelyn, who had just received her GCSE results. It had been a long journey with many battles waged to get to this place, for Katelyn herself and for us as a family. Earlier that week, Katelyn and I had talked about wanting to praise God and to give Him the glory for His amazing part in her story. I had planned to write some things down for the following Sunday. However, as I stood worshipping God that morning, I felt like I would burst if I didn't say something. We were singing about God being an amazing God, when suddenly I had an overwhelming sense that it was the right time to go to the front of the church and share with others what had happened.

We discovered after the meeting that several people had been moved to tears to hear some of what God had done, both those who knew part of her story and those who had heard it for the first time. There were some visitors amongst the congregation that morning and my eyes were drawn to one lady in particular. As I spoke, I noticed that she was visibly moved by what I was saying and at the end of the meeting she sought me out, took my hands in hers and thanked me with tears in her eyes, which made me wonder what my story had meant to her. I sensed that God had particularly wanted this lady to hear our testimony and that this could be the reason I had felt compelled to speak that morning. It was the only time she visited the church.

The effect the testimony had on other people's hearts left me with a desire to tell the whole story. I realised that, as well as glorifying God, the story gave others hope and built faith that the God of the Bible is still the God of miracles and is at work amongst us here and now.

After I shared the testimony that morning with the congregation, there was a new prophetic word given about Katelyn by Paul Johnson.

He said that her name meant 'pure' and he went on to share the scripture from Matthew 5, verse 8:

"Blessed are the pure in heart for they shall see God."

Katelyn had already seen God work miraculously in her life and Paul prophesied that God would continue to do more in the future.

We have certainly continued to see God at work in our daughter and she has accomplished things which we believe she could not have done without His abiding presence in her life. Phil and I had been given limited expectations of Katelyn's educational potential early on in her life. At each stage, we have been amazed to see God take her on to achieve more.

During the last year of her A level studies, Katelyn had decided she wanted to go on and study at university. She applied to three performing arts courses and was, in due course, invited for auditions at all three. She went on to pass these and was offered places at each, subject to grades. Having visited each of her options a couple of times, Katelyn settled on Buckinghamshire New University at High Wycombe as her first choice, and started her studies there in September 2014.

Once Katelyn expressed a desire to go to university and we could see the potential to do so, we were a hundred percent behind her decision. Although we knew it was an ambitious choice for someone with her learning difficulties and Asperger syndrome, we believed that it would also be a unique opportunity for her to gain life skills and learn how to live independently.

Many youngsters struggle with the challenging step of independent living alongside studying for a degree, even when they don't have any learning difficulties or disabilities to handle. For our daughter, it was a huge mountain, but one she was determined to climb. Asperger syndrome affects people differently. For her, the condition meant that she found change scary, and in one go she was about to change just about everything in her world. Her Asperger condition also meant that she had experienced difficulty making friends in the past and had been bullied at primary and secondary school. She still found crowded places like supermarkets stressful at times because of the noise and the numbers of people around her; she would describe experiencing this as a sensory overload.

Despite all the potential difficulties that faced Katelyn as she stood on the brink of university life, there was one important thing in her favour: she had a robust faith of her own in God and her trust was in Him. This made all the difference to her, and to us, in letting her fly from the nest and into independent life. Her life had not been easy, yet here was a young woman who had learned that she had value and significance in the eyes God and that He loved her beyond measure. She had confidence in Him through her experiences and knew that He would be with her in everything she did and wherever she went.

In spite of the hurdles she has faced, God has provided everything Katelyn has needed to overcome each situation or difficulty she has encountered and she has grown stronger in it. We recently attended a public performance of the play "Queen of the Skies", devised and co-written by Katelyn and one other student. She also performed one of the lead roles in the successful production, which was based on the life of the aviator Amelia Earhart. The play was the culmination of months of group-based work in a theatre company called "Forgotten Dreams"; a very real challenge which demonstrated the growth Katelyn has made.

During her time at High Wycombe, Katelyn has been blessed to have a network of lovely friends who have cared for and encouraged her, including two wonderful student workers (Ida and Nicola) from King's church. She has also been mentored and encouraged by Jen, the worship leader of the band Katelyn plays bass guitar with. Her cousin Clara, another student in High Wycombe, was an additional source of support, and the Student Group at King's church as well as the Christian Union at Buckinghamshire New University have been central in Katelyn's life at university. As Secretary of the C.U. she has been involved in arranging various projects to witness God's love to fellow students.

As she leaves High Wycombe later on this year, we are in anticipation of the next step in God's plan for Katelyn's life.

Although much of my story has concentrated on Katelyn, due to the remarkable things we have seen God do in her life, we have also witnessed our son grow into a man whose life has been lived for and moulded by God. Like his younger sibling, Chris has a robust faith of his own, which began from an early age.

Chris's premature start and low birth weight caused no lasting difficulties for him. From early on, it was clear that he was a high achiever academically. From primary school, having passed the Kent test, Chris went on to grammar school, where he did well in maths and science related subjects. Whilst at secondary school, he became involved with the Christian Union group there and by the time he left, he was using his precocious people skills and maturity to run it. At eighteen, he went to Loughborough University, from which he graduated with a Bachelor of Engineering Degree.

Once at university, Chris chose the New Frontiers church in Loughborough as his place of worship, along with Rachel, a fellow student he had met during the first weeks he was there. Soon Rachel was introduced to us as his first girlfriend.

From the start, it seemed to us that this was just one of those relationships engineered by God. Being a year older than Chris, Rachel had applied to Loughborough twelve months earlier. However, Rachel deferred her entry, in favour of a gap year, which meant they both arrived there in September 2006. Following a short engagement, in July 2008 Chris and Rachel were married.

Rachel went on from gaining a Master of Engineering Degree at Loughborough University, to qualify and work as a Primary School Teacher. Chris is working for Rolls Royce as a Materials Engineer in their Civil Large Engines division. He is also undertaking a Research Degree at Imperial College London in connection with his job.

Chris and Rachel continue to play an active role in their church, serving in areas including worship, trustees and running a small family-oriented group. They are expecting their first child later this year.

We continue to see the God of miracles at work...

What Shall I Read Next?

My Mighty Son

Virág Wheeler-Mezei

ISBN 978-1-911086-54-3

"This is the story of a journey that few of us have to take; it is only for the bravest. When Luki was born to Virág and James, he seemed a very healthy baby. And then their lives changed suddenly and drastically. Luke became unwell at around six months old. He was admitted to the local hospital and then was transferred to Bristol for radical emergency brain surgery for an aggressive brain tumour…

"But this is a story of triumph in the midst of pain, frustration, bewilderment and uncertainty; of peace and confidence where normally there would be none."

- Rev. Patrick Whitworth

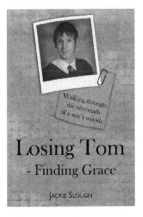

Losing Tom, Finding Grace

Jackie Slough

ISBN 978-1-907509-07-0

Written as a journal it is an honest and intimate revelation of one woman's ability to cope with the unexpected suicide of her teenage son.

Tom was a deep-thinking and creative young man, and an active Christian. How can a young Christian commit suicide? How can a parent not feel condemned? What goes through the minds of people in these circumstances? Excerpts from Tom's Diary are included.

You will find it difficult to put this book down. As you read through the emotional honesty of this narrative you will wonder at God's amazing grace.

Books available from all good bookshops or from the publisher:

www.onwardsandupwards.org